CHRISTIAN FAITH
AND MY EVERYDAY LIFE

Robert Faricy S.J.

Christian faith and my everyday life

The spiritual doctrine of Teilhard de Chardin

St Paul Publications

St Paul Publications
Middlegreen, Slough SL3 6BT
Great Britain

Copyright © St Paul Publications 1981

Published November 1981

Printed by the Society of St Paul, Slough

ISBN 085439 197 5

*St Paul Publications is an activity of the priests and
brothers of the Society of St Paul who promote the
christian message through the mass media*

Contents

Preface

Every great Christian thinker emphasises some great Christian mystery and makes it central to his thought. Thomas Aquinas stressed the mystery of the Trinity. Karl Rahner stresses the Incarnation. The religious writings of Pierre Teilhard de Chardin find their roots in the mystery of the Second Coming of Jesus Christ at the end of the world.

Teilhard de Chardin's understanding of Christ's Second Coming has the world moving towards Jesus Christ. Not so much that the risen Jesus will come; rather, that this troubled world is moving towards him. And when the trajectory of world history is over, God will intervene, Jesus will appear again to take the world definitively to himself in the final judgement, and at last God will be all in all. For Teilhard, the stable point is Jesus Christ, and the world moves towards him. He is the future focal point of the convergence of all that moves forward in this world. And God's plan is that all things finally be reconciled under one head, Jesus Christ.

This same Jesus Christ, the future focal point of each of us and of the whole world, not only stands at the world's end — ahead

7

of us in the ultimate future — but he stands present to each of us and to the whole world in this present moment. The whole world, and each one of us individually, holds together in — and because of — the loving presence of Jesus Christ.

Jesus risen, then, is my future and he is also my present.

This small book tries to clarify for Christians today the meaning of the principal insights of Teilhard de Chardin. The aim of the book is the same as the aim of Teilhard's own writings: to show more clearly the meaning of Jesus Christ so that we can live more fully in him.

There is an urgency in the spiritual doctrine of Pierre Teilhard de Chardin. He wants to sound an alarm, to waken us to the fact that the Day of the Lord, the end of the world, is not only coming; it is already present in a hidden and mysterious way in the Person of He-who-comes. Jesus risen stands and walks among us, drawing us to himself, giving us his life.

Blow the trumpet in Zion;
sound the alarm on my holy mountain!
Let all the inhabitants of the land tremble,
for the Day of the Lord is coming, it
    is near.

(Joel 2, 1)

Jesus said to her, "I am the resurrection
and the life; he who believes in me, though
he die, yet shall he live, and whoever lives
and believes in me shall never die".

(John 11, 25-26)

*　　*　　*

Parts of this book have appeared, in slightly
different form, in *The Teilhard Review,
America, Religious Education,* and *The Tablet.*
I want to thank Sister Lucy Rooney S.N.D.,
and Father John Navone S.J., for reading the
manuscript and making suggestions, and Mrs
Leslie Wearne for typing it. And I want to
thank in a special way Sister Ida Peterfy
S.D.S.H., for her ideas and encouragement.

ROBERT FARICY S.J.

Rome
The Feast of the Transfiguration, 1981

1

The meaning today
of Teilhard's life and thought

One of the century's greatest Christian thinkers was Father Pierre Teilhard de Chardin, the Jesuit priest-paleontologist whose writings have so greatly influenced Catholic thought in the quarter century since his death. His religious ideas gave rise to an official warning (*monitum*) from the Vatican's "Holy Office" in 1962; helped to structure the doctrine of *Gaudium et Spes,* Vatican II's Pastoral Constitution on the Church in the Modern World; and provided the principal ideas for much contemporary theology of original sin, of Christian involvement in the world, of prayer, and of human progress. Further, Teilhard's spiritual teaching, especially as he expressed it in writings such as *Le Milieu Divin* and *Hymn of the Universe,* has touched the hearts and lives of thousands of Christians.

Does Teilhard still speak to us? Does he address our real problems today? Can he help us now? What does his life and thought mean today? Here is what it has meant to me.

Having taken the night train from Auster-

litz Station in Paris, arriving in Clermont at
five-forty on Sunday morning, I wait in the
train station a while and then walk through
the early morning streets to the twelfth-century
church of Notre Dame du Port. I arrive just
before the first Mass. The church, like the sky
now and like the whole town, wears a sombre
grey, the colour of solidity, of moderation and
compromise, the colour of the rocks and stones
that the boy Pierre Teilhard de Chardin found,
collected, and compared when the Teilhard
family lived outside the city in the spring,
summer, and early autumn. But at this time of
year, mid-November, they would have been
back in town for the cold winter months,
attending Mass at this same church, perhaps
the early Mass.

There are few people: some elderly ladies,
a few older men, two or three families. The
Mass is perfunctory. Pierre Teilhard de
Chardin was born in this grey town, went to
this grey church, grew under this grey sky.
Formed in a middle-class family, in a middle-
class Catholic piety, how could he here have
somehow ingested the seeds, the early begin-
nings of his particular Christian vision with
its newness and its brightness?

Christian faith and everyday life

The key to Teilhard's thought, it occurs to
me now in this church, is here, in this very
greyness. Teilhard's originality had its roots in

his unsentimental moderateness, in his quite traditional personal piety, in his conservative need for balance and harmony and a unified vision. His genius and his gift was to make startling sense out of our everyday faith lived out in our workaday world, to light up our humdrum existence so that we are shocked into seeing its meaning. Teilhard understood, and teaches us, the extraordinariness — in the light of faith — of the ordinary. And he began to learn it here, in this so ordinary context.

After Mass, and after a cup of coffee, I wait at the train station for the ten-thirty train to take me to Lyon, where Teilhard's life, soon after his death, intersected with mine. The train passes through Vichy and arrives at Lyon at one-thirty. The city is quiet; Lyon is a Sunday afternoon kind of town, strong on family life and good food.

I studied theology here, at the seminary on Fourvière, the hill that looks down on the city with its two rivers and the rainbow-mist they somehow create. At Lyon-Fourvière, studying with the Jesuits of Teilhard's own Lyon Province of the Society of Jesus, I learned to think, to work with ideas. And I met Teilhard's writings.

At the time, in 1960, Teilhard was controversial, not so much for his published writings as for the essays that circulated in carbon copies, passed from hand to hand, especially among Jesuits in Northern Europe and in France. In 1962, the Holy Office would

13

issue a *monitum,* a warning to Catholics that Teilhard's writings could lead them into doctrinal error; and Teilhard's works, those that had been published so far, would be removed from the library shelves open to the Jesuit seminarians of Lyon-Fourvière. But in 1960, I could read him. The first paragraphs I read spoke to me, reflected back to me my own deepest intuitions, put into words for me what I already knew dimly but had never formulated conceptually. Teilhard's sentences spoke to me with a force that no other philosophy or theology had ever had for me. That force was and still is a force that integrates meanings into an overall synthesis so that I can understand myself, my place in the world, and all my relationships including my relationship with God, in one vision, as one integrated whole.

Later on, after I was ordained, I spent three months in Paris while Father Christopher Mooney S.J., was writing his doctoral thesis — the first ever written on Teilhard's thought — for the Institut Catholique. On afternoon walks, Father Mooney talked, and I learned about Teilhard. Christopher Mooney had discovered Teilhard's unpublished essays, the bulk of his religious thought, and he shared with me not only Teilhard's insights but his own enthusiasm.

To finish my theological studies, I went to the Catholic University of America in Washington, D.C. One sunny spring afternoon, doing research for my doctoral thesis on the

doctrine of Saint Thomas Aquinas' *Comment-
ary on the Sentences of Peter Lombard* regarding the soul's metaphysical relationships through
grace with the three Persons of the Holy
Trinity, examining the thought of Capreolus,
Saint Thomas's earliest commentator, I sud-
denly sat straight up on my library stool, closed
the heavy tome, and asked myself why I was
studying something that did not speak straight
to me in terms of my own experience. I had
already written sixty pages of the thesis, but
that evening I changed topics. I decided
to write on Teilhard de Chardin's theology of
the Christian in the world; the decision
changed my life.

Christopher Mooney helped me greatly in
collecting Teilhard's published works and
copies of his unpublished essays. As I read and
assimilated them and tried to make Teilhard's
vision my own, I found my whole perspective
shift and become more coherent. My interior
life changed, deepened. I became more aware
of who I am, of what I am doing in this
world, and of who Jesus Christ is for me.

In particular, I gradually came to see with
great clarity that the central relationship in
my life is my relationship with Jesus Christ
risen, and that this relationship has priority
over everything else, is "the one thing
necessary" and "the better part" (Luke 10, 42).
Further, Teilhard taught me that this central
relationship with Jesus risen, this central axis
of my life, gives meaning to all my other

15

relationships, organises them, brings them into harmony, gives them life.

Theology and experience

My purpose in this first chapter is to show how the life and thought of Teilhard have influenced my life, as a way of showing his possible importance for the lives of others. How can another person's spiritual teaching help me? The written teachings of all the great spiritual writers — one thinks of Augustine, of Teresa of Avila and John of the Cross, of Thomas Merton — have recorded the writers' own experiences. Teilhard's spiritual teaching stands as the formulation of his religious experience.

The "problem of the two faiths" that Teilhard sees as the principal religious problem of our age was first of all Teilhard's personal problem: how can one person who believes both in God and in the world reconcile these two apparently opposed beliefs?

And the solution that he proposes is the one he found for himself: Jesus Christ risen as personal centre of synthesis. By living out fully his vocation as a Jesuit priest and at the same time immersing himself in his studies and research, he learned that the God of the above and the God of the forward are identical. God has willed, in Jesus, to become involved in the world. And in the risen Christ, the world finds a future focal point for its progress. Jesus risen draws the world to himself, reconciling all things in himself; and Teilhard, in performing his duties and in so contributing in his own small way to the world's forward movement, came to recognise that in doing so he was moving and moving the world around him, closer to the reconciliation of all things in Christ.

Knowing something of Teilhard's life-experience and of his writing has helped me to understand my own central religious problem and, like Teilhard, to find the solution by trying to centre my life always more fully on the risen Jesus. Teilhard has taught me by his life and his writings that there is more to my life than a face-to-face relationship with Jesus Christ in my Mass and in my personal prayer. There is a side-by-side relationship with the Lord in even my most mundane activities, because all that I am and do can be, should be, brought into the zone of my relationship with Jesus. Everything I do has a properly religious significance because I can do it in Christ.

I see more clearly the meaning of my life, including the meaning in my most banal encounters, actions, interests. The meaning is given from the future towards which every day and every minute moves me. That future Jesus Christ holds in his hands. My future lies hidden from me, and I do not know what it holds; but I know who holds it. Present to me now, the risen Jesus makes present my future hidden in him. And so he is the ground of my hope, my assurance that my life as well as the life of the world will have an ultimately successful outcome.

This, of course, is how all philosophy and

theology should work, although they seldom do. The writer describes and formulates his own experience, reflecting on that experience. I use his formulation to express to myself my own experience. I assimilate his concepts in my own life experience, and so I can speak my own experience, my life and my identity, better to myself. In this way, I am able to live in a more aware way, seeing new meaning. My experience, deepened through awareness, becomes fuller and richer, more meaningful and so more human.

When, as in the case of Teilhard's teaching, the meaning of human experience lies in a person, in the person of the risen Christ, then the greater assimilation of that meaning results in a greater personalisation of one's life. My life becomes not only more humanised but more personalised in Christ. In him, I grow as a person.

Prayer and reflection

In the spring of 1976, having heard for several years of the existence of some notebooks that Teilhard had kept for himself — notebooks containing spiritual points from his annual retreats and reflections on his reading — I went to Paris to try to track them down. I found them easily. Many of Teilhard's notebooks have been lost, but several of those that remain are kept in a locked drawer in an ancient desk in the Jesuit house at Chantilly, north of Paris. Copies of a few of these notebooks can be found in the files of the Teilhard de Chardin Foundation in Paris. But the originals, in Teilhard's own handwriting, remain buried, inaccessible even to scholars. As a special privilege I was allowed to read them after giving my word that I would not take them out of the house or photograph the pages.

I could stay at the Chantilly house only three days, and then I had to travel back to Rome where I teach theology. So it came about that I spent three quite full days, skipping several meals and some sleep, poring over Teilhard's notes and furiously taking notes of my own, for over fifteen hours a day, hidden away in a small room on the top floor of the complex of connected buildings that form the Jesuit centre at Chantilly. I could do only so much in the limited time. I skimmed the notebooks in which Teilhard had copied quotations from books and articles that he read and recorded his reactions to his reading, taking notes myself on what I felt was particularly important.

Most of the time I devoted to the retreat notebooks. I felt as though I were Teilhard's spiritual director, or giving him a retreat. Reading the notes that he had jotted down for his own eyes only, I felt that I was finally meeting the real Teilhard, the essence of the man. It was an experience I find difficult to describe.

Each year, like every Jesuit for centuries, Teilhard took eight or ten days to make the

Spiritual Exercises of Saint Ignatius of Loyola. These Exercises follow a definite pattern, so that the same meditations are made every year without much variation in the structure of the retreat. As a Jesuit, I make the same Spiritual Exercises annually that Teilhard did. So I could enter with ease and understanding into what he had written down during his own annual retreats. Furthermore, the importance of the Spiritual Exercises for a Jesuit cannot be overestimated. They are our "rule". Every religious order has its "rule of life". The Benedictines have the rule of Saint Benedict, the Franciscans and the Dominicans have their "rules". We Jesuits have the Exercises of Saint Ignatius of Loyola. They concretise and sum up for us our whole spirit, our motivation and aims, our way of life.

This means that the retreat notes I read at Chantilly were reflections on a basic experience that Teilhard de Chardin and I shared and that all Jesuits share. I found it easy to enter into Teilhard's reflections and feelings, into his experience. I met the man at a new level, more personally and more movingly.

In a few days, reading through all the retreat notes for the latter part of Teilhard's life, I found myself able to trace certain lines of development in his experience of God, and I was able to distinguish the constant factors in his spiritual life from the variables. The constant element that stood out for me was Teilhard's consistent devotion to the heart of Jesus

20

Christ risen. The variable that impressed me the most was his evolving attitude towards his own death.

The religious experience that lay at the base of the whole edifice of Teilhard's thought was the devotion to the Sacred Heart of Jesus that he learned from his mother and, later, at school from his Jesuit teachers. Personal attachment to the heart of Jesus is the seed of Teilhard's Christology which, in turn, forms the most substantial part of his religious thought. But Teilhard's expression of his understanding of the Sacred Heart grew over the years as his understanding grew. In his retreat journals from 1939 to 1955, the year of his death, he expresses his attachment to the heart of Jesus Christ in terms that contain no echoes of the closed-in sentimentality or the emotionalism and superficiality sometimes associated with the devotion to the Sacred Heart.

The Sacred Heart, for Teilhard de Chardin, is "the personal heart of the cosmos" (1943 retreat, first day), the heart of the heart of the world. Teilhard's love for the heart of Jesus, long before Teilhard studied theology, had begun to synthesise in his own heart his "upward" impulse towards God and his "forward" impulse towards the world, towards the future-to-be-built. And, in his later life, his love for the risen Jesus seen according to the symbolism of the heart of Christ served to unify Teilhard's prayer life and his work of research and writing.

Going through the retreat journals chronologically, I found an increasing emphasis on death. Particularly when Teilhard meditated on the meaning of the cross, he prayed about his own forthcoming death. In his later years, the meaning of the cross for him personally in his retreat notes is, above all, that it represents his own ageing and his own death as a sharing in the passion and death of Jesus.

And yet, the real fear of death as a possible dead end somehow never diminished in the slightest Teilhard's faith in Jesus Christ and that he would be met by Christ after his death. In his last retreat, he writes of "Communion through death". The ultimate and dominating meaning of death is that it is the final passage to new life in Christ.

These two components of Teilhard de Chardin's spirituality, read in the light of his overall spiritual vision, could not but have an effect on my spiritual life. To discover that, truly and in a profound way, Teilhard's philosophical and theological ideas are rooted in a personal and devout attachment to the heart of Jesus Christ risen was, to begin with, at least something of a surprise. A further surprise was to learn how unified were Teilhard's personal spiritual life and his writings for publication. He lived his books and essays before he wrote them down for others.

These facts edify me, help me in my own teaching and writing, in my own relationship with Jesus Christ, and in understanding and living my life as an integrated totality.

Knowing about Teilhard's fear of death and of the unknown beyond death helps me, and can help anyone, to face fear in any form it takes. Fear in our time usually takes the shape of fear of the future, fear of what might happen, of how things might turn out. Teilhard could face his fear of the future, his fear about his forthcoming death, because of his hope in Jesus Christ.

That hope was certainly not optimism, and above all not blind optimism. Teilhard's hope in the risen Christ consisted entirely of his faith relationship with the person of Christ. He lived, and in particular he prayed, in the darkness of faith. But the faith and the relationship were real. Teilhard, towards the close of his life, moved forward by the energy of a faith-based hope.

The photographs of Teilhard in his last years showed a peace, a gentleness, and a tranquillity that one does not find in the photographs taken in the years soon after his ordination to the priesthood. What Teilhard's retreat notes tell us is that the mature peace in Teilhard's face came not from satisfaction with himself or with his work; nor did that peace come from the absence of fear and anxiety. Teilhard's peace came from his personal relationship with Jesus Christ.

Spiritual doctrine as life model

I suggest that the reason for Teilhard's impact on my life and on so many lives is that

23

his spiritual teaching — coming forth from his own experience — speaks to our experience. It gives us a way to understand ourselves and our world in the light of the Gospel. It helps us to enter into loving relationship with the risen Jesus, and to do it right where we are, in and through the world we live in. Teilhard's spiritual teaching, the teaching presented in *The Divine Milieu* and in *The Heart of Matter*, for example, gives us a contemporary way to live the teachings of Jesus, and to find our way, with his help, to a closer union with him in and through the world.

Prayer for understanding

Lord Jesus, teach me your ways. Help me to know you better, to love you more, to follow you more closely. Teach me to see myself and the world around me in the light of your love for me and for the world.

You know my name; you knew it before my birth, before my conception, before the beginning of time. You know me through and through, perfectly, every thought, feeling and action. Every hope and every discouragement. My joyful moments and my failures. My past, my present, my future.

And you accept me totally, just as I am. You affirm me in my personal identity. You teach me to see more clearly.

Lead me, Lord Jesus, to see more clearly

24

your place in my life. Help me to understand better myself and the world I live in. Shine the light of your love for me on me and on my personal situation in the world.

Lord, that I may see.
Amen.

2

The importance of love

In a changing world, the word of God must continually be brought to a new expression, must be adapted and re-adapted to diverse cultures and to new generations. This does not mean that God's word should be distorted to suit the hearers. It means simply that his word must be addressed to people.

Pierre Teilhard de Chardin, the Jesuit priest-scientist who stands out as the most creative Catholic thinker of this century, had as his life-goal the bringing-to-expression of God's word in the thought patterns and categories of the twentieth century. He regarded his work as a beginning, not as a finished synthesis. He saw his ideas as tentative, open to correction and further development, subject to critical reflection. This makes it comparatively easy to adapt and to apply his ideas today more than a quarter of a century after his death.

Particularly important today is Teilhard's effort to rethink the mystery of creation in terms of human progress and of the unification of human society through love. Teilhard understands true human progress as a co-operation with the Creator, a further-creating of the world towards the final reconciliation of all things in Christ. And this co-operation with God-creating, this continuous building up of the world, takes place through love. Love, for Teilhard, is the force and the energy of human progress.

In recent years, even in Christian circles, stress falls often on justice rather than on love. In part, this contemporary emphasis on justice and on the struggle for justice derives from the Marxist theory of class struggle and the revolution of the oppressed proletariat. This chapter briefly compares Teilhard's view of progress through love with the Marxist view of progress through class conflict; and it concludes by pointing out some affinities between Teilhard's thought and the encyclical of Pope John Paul II, *Rich in Mercy* (*Dives in Misercordia*, 1980).

Teilhard de Chardin: Love and creation

The simplest way to consider Teilhard's view of human progress, in order to compare it with the general Marxist view, is to describe his theology of creation. Teilhard rethinks the traditional Thomist creation theology.

For several centuries, Roman Catholic theology has understood creation metaphysically, following the thought of Saint Thomas Aquinas. Saint Thomas describes God's creative act as creation from nothing, out of nothing. This is a metaphysical concept, not an historical one. *All* creatures are created out of nothing, not just the first creatures; and all creatures are created out of nothing at this moment, not only at the beginning of their existence. Thomas's question is: Why is there something instead of nothing? His answer is that God holds things in existence at every instant, makes them be, creates them continuously. "Creation is not a change, but the very dependence itself of the created being on the principal which produces it" (*Contra gentiles,* IIa, c. 18). Creation understood as the creature's dependence on the Creator who holds it in existence and keeps it from falling into nothingness is creation as a kind of vertical relationship. God *is* existence itself, and so — just as fire sets aflame what it touches — God makes things exist; every creature, while a being in its own right, can be seen as a "flaming up" of God. This is a Christian world-view for a contemplative and eternity-oriented age.

Teilhard keeps the idea of creation as continuous. And he tries to rethink the Christian doctrine of creation in contemporary categories of thought in such a way that the Christian can integrate his or her Christian faith with everyday experience. He understands creation not as a divine act at the beginning of time, nor as a relation in the creature to its Creator, but as a continuous process which is perceived by us as history, as the forward movement of each and every thing in time. In other words, Teilhard understands creation as the on-going continuous process of the gradual recapitulation of all things in the risen Christ. Creation is that great process of unification by which God draws all things into a unity in Christ. We perceive and live this process as the world's historical movement into the future.

In this way, Teilhard understands creation as creation in and through Jesus Christ. Creation is still a relationship, but now it is a "horizontal" and dynamic relationship with the Creator who — from the future, as it were — draws all things to himself in Christ. God's work of the continuous creation of the world is expressed in the world as a gradual historical process that converges on Christ. This is a Christian world-view for an active and future-oriented age.

If creation is a process of creation in Christ, then I can contribute to it. Whatever I do in the line of unification, of reconciliation, of love, is my contribution to bringing all things together in Jesus Christ. I am a co-creator, in my own small way, with the Creator. This, for Teilhard, is where love comes in. I co-create through love. My loving is creative; it co-operates with God's plan of creation.

Love is the great unifying force. What binds creatures together is love. The interior mutual attraction that runs all through nature, that binds particles to make atoms, atoms to make molecules, cells to make bodily organs and whole bodies, when found at the level of human consciousness is what we call love. Love binds us together by a free mutual adhesion that comes from the interior.

Teilhard's theology of creation, and in fact all his philosophy and theology, presuppose the primacy of the future as well as the future convergence of all lines in Christ. In his thought, therefore, there is stress given to action that unifies and to love which is the bond of unity.

Traditional Catholic theology has, since the time of Thomas Aquinas, been — like Thomas and chiefly because of him — intellectualist. It has emphasised the primacy of the human intellect over the will; I choose what I know as good and to-be-chosen. If I sin, it is because I talked myself into it; I rationalised and so chose a wrong as though it were right. I can face (intellectually) the error of my ways, and so have a conversion of heart. The will follows the intellect, does what it presents as to-be-done. Because of this primacy of the intellect, our highest activity is contemplation, and in heaven we will have the (intellectual) Beatific Vision and therefore love God with our whole hearts. The purpose of all philosophy and theology is that we may better know the truth.

For Teilhard, love has the primacy. He follows the traditional minority opinion in Western Catholic thought, represented by John Duns Scotus and the Franciscans in general, that gives more importance to the will, to action, to love. If I sin, it is mainly because I want to, and therefore I talk myself into sinning. Intellect and will interact in a complex process, but what matters in the end is what

I want, choose, love. Teilhard is interested not only in love of truth, but above all in the truth of love, in the meaning that God's love in Christ gives to the world.

The dialectic of man and nature

Before considering Marxist theory specifically, it seems well to describe dialectical process in general. Dialectical process is the movement in time produced by the tension between two related elements — for example, man and nature. This tension or polarity is a relationship in which there is always some kind of opposition between the two elements. However, the two opposed elements can be related in two different ways. The two elements can complement one another in a fruitful relationship; in this case, although one element somehow dominates the other, the relationship is one of complementarity. This is true ideally of the relationship between man and nature.

The other way in which the two opposed elements in a dialectical process can be related is in the classic master-slave relationship; here, the dominating element uses and exploits the other element. These two dialectical relationships, complementarity and master-slave, are the two fundamental polar relationships and mainsprings of all dialectical movement.

Ideally, man and nature are not in a relationship of master and slave but rather in one of complementarity. Man dominates nature in a complementary way, and the union is a

31

fruitful one. In his working union with nature, man becomes more human, develops his own humanity. His union with nature is a humanising union.

In any positive or complementary union, the elements united are always differentiated. Whether we speak of cells united to form a living body, or of members of a human society, or of the elements that make up any union, true union never confuses the elements united, it differentiates them. On an athletic team, players are differentiated according to the positions they occupy on the team; union differentiates. In friendship, there is, again, a a differentiating union. At an even deeper level, marriage is a differentiating union. To the extent that a marriage is a happy and successful union, husband and wife grow as persons. They do not merge or confuse their personal identities; on the contrary, each achieves his or her own personhood — not in spite of the daily lived-out marriage union — but precisely through union with the other person. The differentiation always takes place at the level of the union. Members of a team are differentiated according to function. Friends are differentiated as persons, personalised. In the union between man and nature, man is united with nature precisely as man, as human, as a rational planner and developer and builder. So, in the dialectical process of man's uniting with nature, working with nature, producing with nature, man himself becomes more human. He transcends his former limitations; he grows; he makes more real his own human essence.

The root of the man-nature relationship is need. Man needs nature, even though he is to some extent alienated from it. This relationship of need is mediated by work; through work, man overcomes his alienation from nature in a complementary and fruitful union with nature. Further, he finds himself in the products of his working union with nature; he seems himself objectified and exteriorised in the results of his work. In his products, he sees himself reflected precisely as human, and so becomes more aware of his own nature. This whole dialectical process of man's union with and work with nature so as to produce results is also a process of man's greater humanisation through both the development and the increasing awareness of his human nature.

Man is in the image of God. He is a creator in the image of the Creator. His task on earth is to exercise dominion over nature. Dominion is God's, but God has mandated man to take care of, work with, develop nature. And in being creative man shares in God's own creativity and becomes more in the image of his Creator; that is, he becomes more human.

The dialectic of master and slave

The dialectical process of man and nature does not exist in a vacuum; it is interwoven with other dialectical processes based on the relationships of society, on the relation of man

33

to man. Man-man relationships can be either positive or negative. Human relationships can be complementary; when they are, there is a working together towards common goals, and something is produced, the fruit of working together. Or a human relationship can be negative. In this case, the relationship is, in some way, one of master and slave. It is not a complementary union but one in which the dominating member uses the other as an object, exploiting the other, and appropriating the fruit or product of the relationship to himself.

If both the human relationships in society and the man-nature relationships in technology and industry are positive, complementary, then there is great harmony. In fact, this never occurs. Man-man relationships in any society are never all complementary; there are always master-slave relationships in which persons use others not as persons, as subjects, but as objects to be manipulated for the greater good of the user. This is the fact of sin.

In the dialectic of master and slave, the "master" is united with the "slave" in a working relationship, the work is done principally by the slave, and the product goes to the master. Where the two dialectical processes meet is at their common point, that of work. In the master-slave dialectic, the work is done by the slave, but he does this work by being in some kind of union with nature, with the material means of production. And this second union is positive, a relationship of complementarity; it is the dialectical relationship of man and nature.

Marxism

Marxist theory uses its understanding of these two dialectical processes, and their mingling at the point of "work", to form one complex dialectical process in order to explain proletarian revolution. In a capitalist system, the proletariat is in relation to the owners of the means of production as slave is to master. The worker works, and the product goes to the owner, except for what is necessary for the worker so that he keep working. But the worker is, in his union with the means of production (fields, tools, equipment, and organizational relationships), in a man-nature dialectical process of complementarity. Thus, he is in a humanising process, becoming man, stronger and more aware. Theoretically at a given point, the worker should be sufficiently strong and enough aware of himself as human to break free from the master-slave relationship, overthrowing the capitalist system in favour of a new social and economic order in which the master-slave dialectic does not dominate in societal relationships.

It is at this point, when the proletariat has through the man-nature dialectic become strong and aware, that the importance of ideology becomes clear. The worker needs to objectify his situation by conceptualising it so that he can understand it. The purpose of

Marxits ideology is that the worker be able to conceptualise his situation and see the possibility of a Marxist revolution.

This, basically, is the Marxist theory of revolution: the proletariat grows strong through working with the means of production ("nature"), becomes aware of its alienated state through (Marxist) ideology, and so liberates itself from its slavery by overthrowing the master class in a class struggle, in a revolution that inaugurates a new order, the rule of the proletariat.

The problem here from a Christian point of view is not, of course, growing strong through union with the means of production. In fact, I have explained it here by using Teilhard de Chardin's principle that union of complementarity — of love in some form — personalises, strengthens the person, helps the person to grow as a person. The problem lies in the ideological concept of class struggle, in the idea of a necessary hostility towards an oppressing class so as to overthrow the system and secure justice. For Teilhard, this ideology is dehumanising and destructive because it goes against love. Any involvement in the world that goes against unity, against building up through free consent, through love, is counter productive.

Teilhard and Marxism

In Teilhard de Chardin's writings, the world finds its centre and its future focal

point in the risen Christ. The Christian, therefore, can enter into loving relationship with
Christ in and through the world, and can love
God and the world — God present in Christ
and the world-centred-on-Christ — with a
unified love.

Teilhard describes the modern religious
problem this way: How can one person who
believes both in God and in the world reconcile
those two beliefs? People of this age do believe
in the possibility of a better world, in the pros-
pect of building a better future, in progress, in
mankind. This "faith in mankind", this "faith
in the world", persists in spite of counter indi-
cations and setbacks to human progress. Even
contemporary anxiety functions in terms of
threats to our future, to the personal and
general enterprise of making this world better
for tomorrow, of planning and preparing for
the future.

This faith in the world, in the future, in
human possibilities, this "horizontal" faith,
enters into apparent conflict with a "vertical"
faith in God. Our forward impulse towards the
future can seem irreconcilable with a certain
upward impulse of worship, of adoration, of
searching for union with God.

The "two faiths" problem, the apparent
divergence of two vectors in the contemporary
human psyche — faith in the world and faith
in God — finds its roots in the dilemma of
Teilhard's own life: how to reconcile his
passionate belief in the world with his Christian
faith? How bring into synthesis that whole side

of his life represented by his scientific career and the other side symbolised by his Jesuit priesthood? In formulating the problem of the two faiths, Teilhard expresses his own experience, his own life-problem. His personal solution is the one he proposes to us: to take the risen Jesus as personal centre of synthesis and of organisation, a personal centre who brings into synthesis our faith in God and our faith in the world.

Teilhard, then, sees man and the world around him in complementarity, in a positive and loving union. The world is personalised in Jesus risen, and I can love him in and through my union with the world around me. But, for Teilhard, this love embraces even those who might persecute me or oppress me, because they too make up part of the world centred on Christ. Teilhard has no room for class struggle, for any union or relationship not *lovingly* entered into. That is one way in which his theology differs from Marxist theory.

In Teilhard's concept of interpersonal relationships, the only truly human bonding force is love. Any union of persons that is imposed from above or is somehow coercive is dehumanising, alienating. But his solution to alienation is not to struggle in a conflict against the oppressor, but to love the oppressor, to look on him not with aggressive hostility but with Christian love and forgiveness. Teilhard's insight is that, without acting from love and in love, a person trying to liberate himself will only go from one form of slavery to another —

because it is only positive, complementary union that frees, personalises, gives growth.

Is this naive? It is Christianity.

Justice and Mercy: Pope John Paul II

Pope John Paul II's encyclical *Rich in Mercy* (*Dives in Misericordia*) presents a strong and inspiring Christian theology of God's mercy. And it presents love, forgiveness and compassion as social and political Christian alternatives to aggression and hostility. Pope John Paul II puts justice at the service of mercy. A just social and political order is to be sought not through a class struggle for justice, but through forgiving love.

In *Rich in Mercy*, the Pope draws attention to the face of the "Father of mercies" (p. 4) and centres his teaching on the mercy of God "made visible in and through Christ", "the Incarnation of Mercy" (pp. 6 and 7). "The present day mentality", the Pope writes, "seems opposed to a God of mercy; the word and the concept of 'mercy' seem to cause uneasiness" (p. 8). Human "dominion over the earth seems to leave no room for mercy" (p. 8). Jesus reveals that Divine Love is present in the world and that it goes out especially to those suffering from social injustice and poverty (pp. 11-12).

After a dense but clear theological analysis of the concept of divine mercy, Pope John Paul II stresses that the contemporary sense of justice is not enough; "programmes that begin from the idea of justice suffer from distortion"

(p. 59); "the desire to annihilate the enemy, to limit his freedom . . . contrasts with the essence of justice" (p. 59). "Justice alone is not enough: it can even lead to the negation and destruction of itself, if *that deeper power, love,* is not allowed to shape human life" (p. 60).

Rich in Mercy depends heavily for inspiration and ideas on Vatican II's Pastoral Constitution on the Church in the Modern World, *Gaudium et Spes.* As a Cardinal, the present Pope was one of the architects of *Gaudium et Spes,* and so it is not surprising that his papal teaching follows its spirit closely. Nor is it surprising that *Rich in Mercy* should have close affinity with the thought of Teilhard — it is well known that Teilhard's spirituality, especially in its broad outlines and its major emphases, formed a major conceptual background for the writing of the Vatican II document.

Repeating partially the doctrine of *Rich in Mercy,* Pope John Paul II in a public audience (February 6, 1981) again pointed out the importance of knowing well the spiritual and psychological realities of contemporary Christians. And he said that three biblical images are particularly fitted and needed today in the light of contemporary problems: the Good Samaritan, the Good Shepherd, and the Father of the Prodigal Son. Teilhard would be in complete agreement; all three are images of God's love for us, and models of the love he calls us to have for one another. And love is the energy of all true human progress.

Prayer for the gift of love

Lord Jesus, give me, in greater fullness, your gift of love.

Help me to grow in my capacity to love, to love you and to love others. Help me to grow in my capacity to receive love, from you and from others. I know, Jesus, that growth in holiness means growth in ability to love and to receive love. Give me a new outpouring of your gift of love.

Unite me more closely to yourself in your love for me. Let your love for me re-create me, form and mould me, personalise me into the person you've always planned me to be.

You teach me that, in personalising union of love with you, I grow in holiness; I learn to love more and to receive love better. So unite me more closely to you.

I open my heart to your great love for me. Let it fill me and nourish me and heal me. Heal me particularly in my capacity to give and to receive love. Give me a new heart.

Now, in this moment, I forgive whoever has hurt me in any way. I accept your gift of merciful love, your gift of forgiveness. You forgave your murderers from the cross; and you give me that forgiveness so that I can use it to forgive all who have hurt me.

I visualise in my imagination, one by one, the persons who have hurt me, physically or psychologically or both. With your help, Lord, I embrace each of them in my imagination;

and I tell each, saying the person's name, "I forgive you".

And in my imagination I see you, Jesus, putting your arms around me, forgiving me, filling me with the merciful love that you feel towards me. I accept your forgiving and healing love.

Amen.

3

The meaning of the cross

Teilhard de Chardin, the priest-scientist who contributed so much to a synthesizing of Christianity and of all that is *naturaliter Christianum* in modern human values, has written that Christianity has become, in human terms, antipathetic. Before, it was feared or persecuted. Today, on the other hand, it is kept at a distance, avoided as an encumbrance. The reason for this, Teilhard adds, is not that Christianity seems too difficult or too spiritual, as some Christians pretend to believe, but that it appears as too small, too narrow, and as hostile to the best aspirations of men. What the world is waiting for is not some kind of compromise between Christian values and humanistic values, a watering-down of Christianity to make it seem easier and more conformed to worldly ideas. The need is for a purer and more elevated presentation of the traditional Christian ideals, for the message of the cross. How can the cross of Jesus Christ stand in today's world as the answer to the questions that people today have in their hearts; how can Christianity preach Christ crucified to today's world?

To begin with, one overridingly important

"sign of the times" commands attention: the drive towards involvement in the world in the direction of building a better future. This drive shows up in diverse but related ways in modern western civilisation: the search for greater human rights and dignity for all groups, peoples, and races; the movements for socio-economic development and for political and economic liberation; scientific experimentation and technological application; efforts towards peace and the unification and solidarity of all men; and above all the increasing awareness of persons that each can and should have better educational and work opportunities, more personal and family security, and greater possibilities for personal development. Can Christianity manifest that these future-oriented and this-world values are fulfilled in the cross?

The problem of the cross's meaning

To approach the question in another way, what does or should the cross mean today within the framework of man's involvement in the future? Raised up on the cross, Jesus draws all men to himself. But, at the same time, the cross remains a stumbling block and, even more, foolishness to unbelievers. The world needs, looks for without knowing what it seeks, a formulation, a theology of the cross — not a theology for the philosophers, but a meaning for mankind, a significance that transcends merely human wisdom and shows it as foolishly weak and inadequate in the light of the cross.

The meaning of the cross regards not only Christianity's word to the world but, and first of all, Christians themselves. To speak to man, Christianity needs to be as fully as possible itself; and, essentially, it is the religion of the cross. The Christian religion has always been pledged to and identified with the cross of Jesus. To live up to its own essence, it is obliged to say the meaning of the cross clearly to itself, and then to those who appear indifferent. Christians, too, belong to the present age, and they think and act in the categories of the times. To speak clearly, even to itself, Christianity cries out for the message of the cross in the perspective of present human culture and values.

The cross of Jesus Christ must be understood as a consequence of the Incarnation and as leading to Jesus' resurrection. By the Incarnation God, in Jesus, has joined himself in a new way to men and through men to the world. The relationship between God the Creator and the world, his creation, is fulfilled, brought to a head, in the Incarnation. Jesus represents, and is, God-for-the-world, God involved in the world, God as part of his own creation. Far from indifferent to man's world, God, by the Incarnation, has entered into a mutuality with it and especially with men by becoming a man. God, infinitely free and self-sufficient by his own divine nature, has willed to need the world he made, to need man to complete the divine plan hidden from the ages but revealed in Christ.

Furthermore, Jesus, in his public life and in a special way in his passion and crucifixion, lived out fully the implications of his Incarnation, taking the form of a servant, even to the point of death on the cross. Far from clinging to his dignity as God, he lived totally his humanity, refusing all offers and temptations to worldly power and glory, identifying himself not only with the prophet Daniel's messianic and triumphant image of the Son of Man who will come on the clouds of heaven but also with Isaiah's suffering servant who gives his life as a ransom for many. Jesus' involvement in the world took the form of service — of service of the Father through obedience, and of service to men by securing their salvation. This is why God raised him up to be the keystone of all reality.

God preordained Jesus from the beginning to be, risen, the future focal point of the world's movement, the goal of all history and true progress. But, in order to be that in his risen life, in order to be the central element of the world, Jesus first had to enter the world through being born, living, and dying on the cross. He descended, through his death, to the heart of the world so that, risen, he could act as the heart of the world.

By his death on the cross, Jesus reconciled all men in himself to the Father. But this reconciliation, accomplished in principle on the cross, works itself out gradually in history towards the end of history when all things will find their definitive reconciliation in Jesus, when Jesus will turn the kingdom over to the Father, and God will be all in all.

Jesus died in expiation and in reparation for the sins of men. This is the "negative" side of the redemptive act of the cross, that Jesus died to save men from their sins. Equally or more important is the positive aspect of the cross. Jesus died to save men not only from sin but to the Father, to the freedom of the children of God, and to life in the Spirit. The death of Jesus must then be understood as primarily a positive act of the conquest of sin and death, the act by which Jesus raised up the world to God, the principal act that saves men.

The meaning of the cross

Understood in this way, the cross of Jesus appears as a symbol and the reality not only of reparation and expiation for sin, but primarily as the symbol and the reality of progress through struggle and suffering and difficult labour. Jesus' death was, in the deepest sense, not a failure but a victory over the powers of darkness, a conquest of sin and death and all that oppresses man, a raising up of the world.

Teilhard de Chardin writes that the cross is "the symbol not merely of the dark and retrogressive side of the universe in genesis, but also and, even more, of its triumphant and luminous side". It is "the symbol of progress and victory won through mistakes, disappointments, and hard work". And it is the cross that

47

we can "offer to the worship of a world that has become conscious of what it was yesterday and what it awaits tomorrow" (*Christianity and Evolution,* p. 163).

This view of the cross emphasises its orientation to Jesus' resurrection and so to the ultimate future that begins in an anticipatory way with the resurrection of Jesus. A positive understanding of the central act of man's redemption stresses the forward and horizontal component of the cross, its relation to history not as a simply historical event but as that event that orders history in the direction of the world to come at history's termination. But it does not at all detract from the vertical or transcendent component of the cross. Jesus' death remains obedience to the Father's will, a total sacrifice of love to God, the action in which the world opens out to the transcendence of God and so to its own salvation. The "forward" component of the cross, its future-directness, and the "upward" component, its relation to God in his transcendence, are brought into synthesis. The God of the "upward" is the God of the "forward". The transcendent God has become, in Jesus, immanent in the world. And Jesus, having died, risen, and taken his place at the right hand of the Father and as the goal of history, centres the world and its movement into the future on himself. Jesus is the God of both the "upward" and the "forward"; in him the "horizontal" and the "vertical" meet in synthesis. The natural order and the supernatural order, while distinct, come together in that integration of natural and supernatural that effects the world's redemption.

In this world, we live in the existential structure of the cross, a cross ordered to the end of time, to the final death and transformation of this world into the world to come, and to our own resurrection. We enter truly into the world moving into the future only to the extent that, somehow, we become involved in the world by entering as fully as possible into the structure of the cross. In *The Divine Milieu,* Teilhard de Chardin points out that

> . . . the royal road of the cross is no more nor less than the road of human endeavour supernaturally righted and prolonged. Once we have fully grasped the meaning of the cross, we are no longer in danger of finding life sad and ugly. We shall simply have become more attentive to its barely comprehensible solemnity (p. 104).

The Christian doctrine of the cross does not deny the value of man's involvement in the world as to-be-built towards a better future. On the contrary, the cross affirms that value and gives it its deepest meaning. We are all called to be disciples of Jesus, to take up our crosses and to follow him. We are called by God to enter fully into the world, as Jesus did, to "descend into" history, to become involved in constructing the kingdom. God does not ask us

49

"to swoon in the shadow, but to climb in the light, of the cross".

We are called, then, to take responsibility for our own lives, for the world, for the future. This responsibility is to be carried out in a sinful world, by taking up the cross of the struggle against the powers of darkness, against all that keeps man down. The cross stands for the struggle against evil, against all that oppresses men. It stands for the struggle for human rights and dignity, for social and economic and political freedom, for freedom from those sinful structures of society that impede us from realising our full God-given potential. And the cross stands for each person's struggle, in a sinful world, to build his own life and the life of the society he lives in. The teaching of the cross calls me to involve myself in the future with an involvement that takes the shape of the service of others in the hope of a fuller life in this world and the fullness of life in the next world. The cross represents the struggle for freedom from sin, from the sinfulness interior to each person and from the objectified sinful structures of human society.

Freedom from death

The sum of all evils, the summation of all that oppresses man, is death. This is why all simple human values, however valid and noble, finally fail: they cannot point to anything beyond death. They find defeat in the end because they end with death. This holds true not just for personal, individual values but also for social values, for the ethical systems of human collectivities, of democratic, capitalist, socialist, fascist, and communist societies. They cannot lead man to ultimate victory, to life beyond death.

The strength of Christian values lies in the saving power of the cross of Christ which represents and which is the triumph over the last enemy and the greatest, death. Contemporary mankind, increasingly aware of its unity and of the fact that it is headed into a future for which it is responsible, faces the unspoken fear of death, not only of the death of the individual but of the death of mankind itself. The moral sickness of contemporary societies has its ontological and psychological grounding in a deeper sickness, in the fear of the death of the human race. This anxiety in the face of extinction, the extinction not just of the individual but of mankind itself, becomes more acute as man grows in the awareness of the future. Where does the future of mankind end? And if all human efforts are ultimately doomed, if mankind itself is moving towards a dead end, what makes the whole human enterprise ultimately worth the effort? If nothing of value can permanently endure as the result of human efforts, then why make the effort? If ethical norms and values finally lead up a blind alley, then why follow them at all?

By his death on the cross Jesus has converted death into a passage to eternal life. Death has been conquered by being transformed into the way to resurrection. Insofar as anyone's death participates in the death of Jesus, takes place in union with him, that death shares in the victory of Jesus' death and leads to eternal salvation. In death, personal existence breaks up completely; death breaks and fragments the personal unity that has been built up during a lifetime. This final and total fragmentation is the necessary condition of the final personal synthesis in which God in Jesus puts the person back together, this time with a new and eternal wholeness, in glory.

The world, too, and all mankind, will, at the end of history, die, break completely into fragments, so that God can rebuild it, transformed into the world to come. Everything of value that we have done or built or endured on earth will be found transformed and purified, burnished, after the world's death and rebirth.

In the same way, our life can be, in Christ, a continuous dying and rising in Christ, a sharing in the paschal mystery. Each cross breaks up the provisory unity of the person, fragments the individual so that — to the extent that the cross is suffered and carried in union with Christ — God can put the pieces back together, this time in a higher synthesis in which the person finds a closer union with God. This is the path of personal spiritual progress.

The Church, too, and every society insofar as it exists in Christ, follows the way of the cross. It lives, suffers, and progresses, moving ahead through the pain of growth, coming apart and then coming together again closer to God. Suffering is, in this world, the price of progress.

Each person, every society, and mankind as a whole, are called to act out, in history, the life, death, and resurrection of Jesus, sharing in those mysteries on the way to the final reconciliation of all things in the risen Christ. All Christian values, then, are integrated and summed up in the cross that leads to new life.

Credibility and the cross

The effectiveness of the Christian message of the cross depends on three factors. First, the message must be intelligible to man today, coherent; and it must correspond to and be seen to be the fulfilment of what is best in contemporary values. Secondly, the cross must be presented as a realistic ideal that can, with the help of God's loving mercy and grace, be lived and actualised. Finally, the message of the cross must be credible.

This can be stated in another way. The cultural changes taking place in the post-Christian western world originate in new perceptions. Man perceives himself as part of the human collectivity moving rapidly into the future. This complexus of perceptions gives rise to a new general cultural vision: that of a progressing society in an evolutionary world. The new vision generates new values: freedom with dignity, opportunity with rights and status, a better human society in the future, the value of an involvement in the world that takes the form of work to build the future. But the increasing perception and awareness of the problem of death threaten the new vision and values, which — in the light of death's inevitability — appear as inadequate and incomplete. This is the problem. The solution is Christianity, which must overcome the religious indifference of contemporary western culture. This can be done only to the degree that Christianity shows itself to have a more adequate vision of reality that completes the modern secular vision, to the degree that it manifests more adequate values that fulfil modern secular values, and to the extent that it does this credibly, to the extent that it presents its vision and its values as to-be-adhered-to, as to-be-believed. The Christian vision and values are embodied in the cross ordered to new life. How can the cross be made credible, witnessed to so that men can believe what it stands for?

It is only to the point that Christianity lives what it says that it will be believed. The First Vatican Council has stated that "the Church itself . . . is a great and perpetual motive of credibility and an irrefutable proof of its own divine mission". Vatican I holds that the Church offers the principal evidence not precisely of the truth that it proclaims — for this can be grasped only in faith — but of the credibility of that truth. In the words of Thomas Aquinas, "man cannot believe unless he sees that he must believe, either because of the evidence of signs, or because of something similar" (II-II, 1, 4 *ad* 2). Christianity itself is the chief evidence of its own credibility, the sign to the nations that God's word of the cross of Jesus is to-be-believed.

The credibility of the cross depends on how the Church lives the cross. The intelligibility, the values, and the credibility of the cross, all depend to a great extent on how the Church lives the meaning and the values of the cross. This fact is rarely appreciated or even considered by Christians. What matters is not how the Church succeeds but *how it fails,* how it suffers, how it endures hostility and opposition, how it lives the conditions of death, how it stands in the structure of the cross of Jesus. History has proved this in communist countries, in Spain, in Africa, in Ireland, and in Latin America, by its verification of the principle that the blood of martyrs is the seed of Christian faith.

The centre, the high point, and the strongest evidence of the cross's credibility is martyrdom. Popular belief in the early Church held that Jesus was the first martyr. The Christian martyr shares in the martyrdom of Jesus and lives even to death, as Jesus did, the meaning and the values of the cross. In an age of religious indifference the Christian martyr dies not so much in defence of the faith as such as in witness to Christian values. Christianity itself, judged irrelevant, seems not worth persecuting. But its values often menace the ethical systems of modern groups and societies. Martyrdom today is and will be most often a witness to some or all of the values that the cross represents. And so martyrdom gives those values credibility.

In Richard Wright's short novel, *The Man Who Lived Underground,* the black murderer comes up from the city sewers where he has been hiding, to confront the Christian congregation as it sings:

> The Lamb, the Lamb, the Lamb
> Tell me again your story . . .
> O wondrous sight upon the cross . . .
>   (*Quintet:* New York, 1956, p. 45).

They cry that he is drunk, filthy, rowdy. "But I want to tell 'em", he says. He is thrown out of church. Trying later to give himself up to the police, he is shot. His Christianity proves too threatening even to Christians, and he becomes a martyr of racial injustice. The policeman who has shot him states, "You've got to shoot his kind. They'd wreck things". Back in the sewers, the Christian criminal dies. "The current spun him around. He sighed and closed his eyes, a whirling object rushing alone into the darkness . . . lost in the heart of the earth" (p. 58).

Christian martyrs, sharing in Jesus' *kenosis,* in his total self-emptying and self-giving in love, descend with Jesus into the heart of the world to become with him the heart of the world. In the death of every Christian martyr, as in the death of Jesus, the contemporary human value of involvement in the world and in the future is fulfilled in the radical future-directedness of the cross to resurrection and to world to come. Further, martyrdom stands for our total dependence on God and for the obedience to God that we are called to. It represents our essential relation to God, the openness of our nature to the transcendent God, the relation which is the basis of all human dignity and freedom. Martyrdom is the completion of what is best in modern human values. Its witness is the strongest evidence of the values of the Christian cross.

Prayer to follow Jesus more closely

Lord Jesus, you tell me that, to follow you, I must take up my cross and walk in your footsteps. Teach me and help me to do this, to take up my cross and follow you.

Bring to my mind now, Lord, the particular cross in my life, the suffering or setback or serious problem that I labour under, that you want me to pray about in this moment.

Help me now, Lord, in this prayer, to face squarely this particular cross in my life, to look at it without flinching at its ugliness.

I give over to whatever anger or resentment I feel when I face this cross in my life. And I put in your hands any tendency to sadness or depression that I feel when I consider my cross. You took on yourself, Jesus, all my anger and resentment, all my sadness and depression, when you suffered and sweated blood in your breakdown in the Garden of Olives. With you, Jesus, I give all my resentment and all my sadness to the Father; and with you I say to the

Father, "Father, not my will, but yours be done".

Just as you accepted your cross, so too, Jesus, I want, with your help, to accept mine. Just as you were obedient to the Father in loving trust, so too I want to trust you and the Father in love and in obedience.

Teach me, Lord, how my cross is my share in your cross. Teach me the redemptive value of my suffering.

Help me to move forward, into the future, without fear, carrying my cross.

I know that you are with me in my suffering, picking up the pieces of me and putting me together always more centred on you. I know that my cross — my share in your suffering — is a cross of healing. I carry it in union with you. And by your wounds, which you carry in your risen and glorified body, I am healed.

Thank you for calling me to be a Christian, to take part in the Church of Martyrs in this epoch, in this present age of martyrs. Thank you for calling me to live in these times of suffering and martyrdom when the Church shares in your cross in so many ways, in so many lives, in so many places.

Thank you because by this cross in my life I share in your death for me and in all the martyrdoms in the past and in the present — in the deaths for you of all the Christian martyrs.

And I praise you, Jesus, because by your holy cross you have redeemed the world.

4

Teilhard and religious education

The general problem of religious education is this: how to help people to integrate their daily experience and their Christian faith. How can God's word be addressed to people so that they can understand and live Christian faith in terms of their own culture, in terms of their own understanding of themselves and the world around them? The catechetical problem, how to address God's word to people today, is precisely the central problem in all the philosophical and religious writings of Father Pierre Teilhard de Chardin. Teilhard's chief interest and his main lifetime occupation was dealing with this problem. As a priest and a scientist he lived at the intersection of two worlds, the world of science and of contemporary scientific culture at its most intense, and the ecclesiastical and theological world of the Catholic Church. He knew the language and the customs and patterns of both these worlds, and he was at home in and loved them both. He was completely a man of his time and completely a man of God. His lifetime concern and effort was to bring people to Christ by helping them to see and so to live out Christianity in terms of today's world.

The problem of religious education

Teilhard de Chardin saw the catechetical problem as the central contemporary religious problem. How can Christianity be proclaimed to man today? The problem comes to this: how can a synthesis be built between the Christian faith and what is best in contemporary human experience?

The formulation that this problem most often takes in the writings of Teilhard de Chardin is that of an apparent opposition between faith in the world and faith in Christ. He calls it the "problem of the two faiths". The problem of the two faiths is the problem of reconciling Christian faith and faith in man, in the future, in the world, in progress, in man's efforts to build up the world. It is the problem of reconciling Christian detachment and contemporary attachment to progress, of reconciling a single-minded pursuit of the kingdom of God with a dedication to this world. How reconcile the doctrine of the cross and belief in the fullest possible development of human potential? How reconcile love of God and love of the world? Is there not possible a union with God *through* union with the world?

The contemporary Christian feels himself torn in two directions. On the one hand, he wants to be a good Christian, and he is moved in the direction of worship, adoration, and faith in Christ. On the other hand, he believes in mankind and in human effort to build up the world, in human progress, in human potential

60

to build the future. Both of these directions seem good and deserving of all his effort, but they seem to be two different directions. There is an apparent conflict between the upward impulse of faith, worship, adoration, and the forward impulse in the direction of faith in mankind, faith in the world, faith in human progress. This apparent conflict between his upward impulse towards God and his forward impulse towards progress results in a spiritual dualism. Most Christians try to go in both directions at once and they limp badly through life never really achieving a synthesis between faith in Christ and faith in the world.

And yet, as Teilhard de Chardin points out, contemporary faith in the world and hope in the future pose questions that can be answered only by Christianity. People today do have faith in the world, but it is a faith that is more and more in crisis. Today, people do have hope in the future, but it is a hope that is more and more threatened. Teilhard de Chardin's effort to outline the main elements of a solution to the catechetical problem takes the form of an answer to contemporary questions: how can we have faith in the world and hope in the future and how can this faith and this hope be maintained?

Teilhard points out that contemporary faith in the world has the characteristics of a religion, of a religious faith. We have discovered the immensity and the unity of the world; we have discovered the vastness of the universe and of mankind, and we have discovered the oneness of the cosmos and the unity of the human species. We have a consistent world view, a view of a world that is headed as a totality towards some future in which we believe. These two, a world view and a faith in the future, constitute the main elements of a religion. Our own times, far from being irreligious, are increasingly religious. The world has never been more religiously fervent, but it is burning now with a new fervour, with a faith and a hope that are bound up with the building of the earth.

This modern faith in mankind, in progress, in the future, is really a hope. People today see reality as the future to be created. They understand themselves as involved in the world as a task of construction, conquest, and unification. Their commitment is to the future — not of some "other world" — but of *this* world.

The modern "religion of earth" is in our own times clearly in a state of crisis. It is obvious today that blind faith in progress cannot stand by itself. A blind hope in human potential is, taken by itself, insufficient. Nazism and Facism are chilling examples to mankind of what blind faith and unsupported hope in man and his ability to build the future can lead to. Modern warfare, social upheavals, poverty, racism, injustice, all remind mankind more and more that something is wrong. Mankind's faith in the world, and its hope in the future, is more and more called into question. We want to believe in the world, but how can we believe in the world that is full of tragedy, injustice, suffering? We want to hope in the future, but how can we hope in a future that is increasingly threatened, a future that may mean even the total annihilation of mankind? How can human faith and hope be validated? What are their presuppositions? What are the conditions of a solid faith and a secure hope in the world and its future?

Faith is relative and, ultimately, relative to persons. In the end I can trust only in another person. If I am to have faith in the world and to continue to have that faith, I must somehow understand the world in personal terms; I must see the world as somehow grounded in the personal. Hope, too, is relative not only to the future, but to persons. If I am to hope, then ultimately I must hope in some*one*. Faith and hope, in other words, presuppose a certain mutuality of persons; they are basically inter-personal attitudes. To believe and to hope means to be mutual-with, and a person can be mutual only with other persons.

The first condition, then, of faith and hope in the world is that the world be understood in personal terms. And so a first question posed by contemporary experience is: how can the world that is moving into the future be seen as rooted in the personal?

Not only does the world need to be seen as grounded in the personal, but it needs to be seen as moving to a future that is somehow assured; and this is the second condition of faith and hope in the world. How do we know that the world has a future at all? There is an indefinable fear that gnaws at the heart of contemporary man, an anxiety about the future of the world that is peculiarly contemporary. The world is becoming both smaller and more complicated, silence and solitude are disappearing, persons are increasingly lost in the largeness and the complexity of institutions. Faced by all the pressures of modern living, men are increasingly fearful. Teilhard de Chardin suggests that the fear that eats away at man's hope in the future is the fear of death — not so much the death of the individual as the death of the species. The fear is that human progress will end in nothing. It is a fear that is a sickness of the dead end, the anguish of feeling shut in.

In the past one hundred years mankind has become more and more conscious of living in a world that is in a state of evolution. The contemporary person is caught up in the evolutionary progress of human society and his fear is that progress will not have a successful outcome. His fear is that human progress is headed for a point of no return, a dead end. Where are we going? It is the awful presentiment that there is a blank wall ahead of us that underlies all the other tensions and fears so typical of our generation. Teilhard often uses the analogy of miners in a mine-shaft. Mankind is like miners who know that there has been an explosion and that the entrance to the mine-shaft has been blocked. Is there a way out? Is the entrance to the mine-shaft completely blocked or is there perhaps an opening through which the miners can reach sunlight and fresh air? Mankind today is afraid that there is no light at the end of the tunnel. Is there a suitable outcome for human progress? The root cause of contemporary anxiety is the fear that the tunnel might be closed. If man is to continue to hope in the future he has to have some assurance, some promise that there is a way out, that there is a successful future outcome. What makes man hesitant and fearful is uncertainty about the future.

The double question posed by contemporary human experience is then: how can the world be understood as personal so that we can have faith in the world; and how can the future be assured as ultimately successful so that we can have hope in the future? This is the contemporary problem of man to which catechesis should be speaking.

Teilhard de Chardin finds that the question of contemporary faith and hope in the world and its future can be answered only by Christian faith and hope in the risen Christ. The world is grounded in Christ risen, centred on him; the world holds together in the person of the risen Christ. The world then is rooted in a person, and man can relate to the world in a personal way because that world is grounded in the person of Christ. Furthermore, the ultimately successful outcome of human progress is assured by Christ risen. The risen Christ at his second coming is the future focal centre of all true progress. The risen Christ is God's promise to man that man's efforts on earth will have a finally successful end. All Teilhard de

E

Chardin's religious thought is centred on the one hand on the problem posed by contemporary faith and hope in the world, and on the other hand by the solution that is faith and hope in Christ risen. It seems well to briefly outline the structure of Teilhard de Chardin's religious thought in order that the question that is man and the answer that is Christ may be seen more clearly in their interrelationship.

The structure of Teilhard's thought

Any Christian theology is worked out in terms of two sources: divine revelation and some systematic framework within which to interpret that revelation. Thomas Aquinas, for example, interprets God's revelation to us in Christ as contained in Scripture and taught by the Church within the framework of the philosophy of Aristotle. Augustine, in his theology, understands Christian revelation in the categories of neo-platonic philosophy. Karl Rahner tries to present an understanding of God's word to us in Christ through interpreting the data of divine revelation within the categories of his own kind of modern Thomism. So too Teilhard de Chardin's theology is based on two sources: Scripture as taught in the tradition of the Church and a systematic framework. The systematic framework that Teilhard uses is a highly elaborated theory of evolution. Within this theory of evolution Teilhard de Chardin develops a theology of Christ, a Christology, of which the central theme is the relationship of the world to the risen Christ. Based directly on this theology of Christ and the cosmos is Teilhard de Chardin's spirituality, a spirituality of union with God in Christ through the world. His thought, then, exists at three distinct but intimately related levels: first, a theory of evolution and human progress; secondly, a theology of the risen Christ as centre of a world in evolution; and, thirdly, a spirituality in which man's upward impulse towards God and his forward impulse towards progress are united and synthesised.

Teilhard's theory of evolution is a general and broad scientific theory. It is not presented as an absolutely true description of reality but simply as a partial and tentative series of connected hypotheses. Teilhard de Chardin's criterion for the truth of a theory is the universal scientific criterion for truth: a hypothesis or theory is true to the extent that it is coherent and to the extent that it is productive of further research and applications. With this in mind, Teilhard tries to construct a theory of evolution that makes as much sense as possible and that is as useful as possible for further reflection. Briefly, Teilhard finds that evolution has a direction: towards greater degrees of material organisation. The world seen as evolving through time seems to be following an axis of increasing material organisation, an axis that extends in time from the appearance of very simple beings to highly

67

organised beings. Plants appeared in time after molecules, animals after plants, and so on. It seems to be a fact that evolution has a direction, that evolution takes place in the direction of producing beings of greater and greater organisation. Teilhard points out that evolutionary progress in material organisation corresponds with progress in consciousness. Organisation and consciousness seem to be proportional and correlative. The universe, then, has a structure and a direction; it is evolving in the direction of greater organisation and correspondingly greater consciousness. After millions of years the evolutionary process finally produced the most highly organised and at the same time the most highly conscious entity so far — the human being.

Evolution does not stop with the appearance of mankind. Evolution continues, and its area of progress is now the human race, the thinking part of the world. Mankind continues to be more and more highly organised in society; mankind progresses in social and political organisation, in technology, in communications, in economic systems. This increasing organisation of mankind corresponds to increasing general consciousness on the part of the human race, increased culture and civilisation. In man, evolution has become conscious of itself. Not only does evolution continue in human society in the direction of increasing organisation and increasing consciousness, but mankind is conscious of its progress. In fact, man's progress depends on his conscious efforts.

What is more, evolution is convergent. Mankind's organisation is always increasing, and so it must be approaching a maximum point in the distant future, a maximum of human organisation and therefore of general human consciousness. This projected maximum point, the extrapolated terminal point of human progress, is what Teilhard de Chardin calls the "Omega point". After a complex and lengthy reasoning process, Teilhard, by hypothesis, identifies Omega with God. He has now incorporated a hypothetical God-Omega into his theory of evolution. But if God exists, then it seems reasonable to suppose that he would — somehow — communicate himself to man. It seems logical that God would reveal his existence and nature to men by means of a revelation. Teilhard de Chardin suggests, still within his theory of evolution, that it is in religions, and particularly in Christianity, that men should look for such a revelation. A helpful image to keep in mind when thinking about Teilhard de Chardin's theory of evolution is the image of a cone; the base of the cone is the beginning of time and the cone's apex is the end of time. Evolution can be thought of as taking place in the shape of the cone. Evolutionary time could be measured from the base in the direction of the cone's apex. The apex of the cone is God-Omega. At this point Teilhard de Chardin's theory of evolution stops and he is ready to move into a theology of Christ.

In the light of Christian revelation Teilhard discovers the focal centre of the world's progress, the God-Omega of his theory of evolution, to be the risen Christ. The centre of convergent evolution and the focal point of the world's forward movement, the new "God of the forward", is the risen Christ — who is, at the same time, the incarnate traditional "God of the upward". The God that Teilhard adores is God incarnate in Christ risen, a God of both the forward and the upward. It is in the risen Christ that Teilhard finds the seeming opposition between faith in progress and Christian faith, between the "forward" and the "upward", resolved. The world is evolving towards a terminal point which is marked by the second coming of Christ. Teilhard's Christology is one that takes into account not only the human and divine attributes of Christ but also those attributes that can be called cosmic and universal. The Christ of Teilhard's theology is the Christ of Saint John, through whom all things are created and who is the personal principle of the existence and order and harmony of the cosmos. The Christ of Teilhard is even more the Christ of Saint Paul, the Christ in whom all things hold together and in whom all things are reconciled. Teilhard's Christ can be called a cosmic Christ; nevertheless the cosmic Christ is the same historical Jesus of Nazareth who has died for man's sins and who is risen to centre man's world on himself. In fact, it is not so much Christ who is cosmic as it is the cosmos that is Christic. The whole world and its future are personalised in Christ.

At a third level of his thought, based on a theology of Christ worked out within the framework of an evolutionary theory, Teilhard constructs a contemporary spirituality. In this spirituality, the most direct route to heaven is not a route that bypasses earth. Heaven is attained through building up of the world, a world greater and more unfinished than we have realised in the past. It is a spirituality of conquest, of building the world in the direction of the future. In *Le Milieu Divin* Teilhard de Chardin presents Christian spirituality as composed of two complementary movements: attachment and detachment, conquests of the world and renunciation of the world. Attachment and detachment, conquest and renunciation, are for Teilhard de Chardin two modes of the same basic Christian dynamism: to be united with God in and through the world. "Attachment" means attachment to the world's progress, an enthusiastic participation in the human effort to build the world towards its transformation at Christ's second coming. This attachment necessarily demands a high degree of detachment. Christian activity and attachment to the world's progress towards Christ-Omega necessarily lead to renunciation of self, to unselfishness. True attachment to the world's forward movement towards Christ is identical

71

with an austere detachment from selfish interests. It is, as any Christian spirituality must be, a spirituality of the cross that leads to resurrection.

This, then, is the structure of Teilhard de Chardin's religious thought: a mysticism of union with God through the world based on a theology of Christ that is worked out within a theory of evolution. What importance does Teilhard de Chardin's vision of the Christian in a world centred on Christ have for contemporary catechesis?

The meaning for religious education

Teilhard de Chardin has two important things to say to religion teachers today. The first is that religious education must be contemporary. In order to be effective, catechesis must begin with human experience; it must be incarnate in contemporary culture. Secondly, Teilhard's approach underlines the fact that Christian catechesis must be Christ-centred. The purpose of catechesis is not the communication of a set of doctrinal propositions, nor is it principally formation in ethical conduct. The basic purpose of Christian religious education is the communication of Christ.

Religious education, if it is to be contemporary and incarnate in the culture of our times, must take into account modern understandings of person, community, and the relationship between person and community.

72

It is true that catechetics has tried in many cases to come to grips with person and community. In some instances, these attempts have come to failure because the notions of person and community used catechetically were not conformed to common understanding of person and community in modern culture. Some recent catechetical efforts, for example, have been based on European, post-World War II, existentialist philosophy and on the phenomenological thought systems of men like Husserl and Heidegger. These philosophical systems are by their very nature and presuppositions static systems; they do not take into account the dynamic qualities of person and community. In a future-oriented culture, the presentation of Christianity in terms of an understanding of person and community that is a static understanding can be and frequently has been disastrous. Any static understanding of person, whether that understanding be existentialist, scholastic, or frankly Thomist, is not a useful understanding for contemporary catechesis.

Contemporary western culture understands person in terms of growth, development, fulfilment; and contemporary culture understands society in terms of progress, in terms of building and moving into the future, in terms of working in a world that is seen as a future with possibilities. These are not static ideas. They are not existentialist concepts that are rooted in an unmoving present, but dynamic concepts that see person and community as moving into a future. If Christian catechesis is to deal with real problems, then that catechesis must be developed in categories of person and community that are dynamic.

Our culture today is future-directed not only in its conception of person and community but in general. We are involved in the world as future-to-be-built, as world-with-possibilities for the future. We are future-oriented, motivated by what is ahead; and it is the future that draws us and moves us to grow and to transcend present limitations in the direction of a better future. We think and act not in static terms, but in dynamic terms of growth, development, process. We lean into the future. This process-orientation must be central to catechesis. Both children and adults today are interested less in "What is it?" than in "How do you do it?" They are interested in who Christ is, but much more interested in how to encounter him. They want less to know what prayer is than how to pray. They want to know not so much what love is as how to love. Religious education can no longer afford to be statically content-centred; it must be dynamically process-oriented. It must teach not so much "what" as "how".

The contemporary person is future-directed, and he is, therefore, pragmatic. He wants to build the world in the direction of the future, and so he is interested in what is useful, in what he can use to build the world. He is interested in what functions, in what works. This pragmatism should infuse religious education.

Catechesis should be process-oriented; and, if it is, content will be used pragmatically, in such a way that it contributes to the learning of processes.

Christian catechesis must not only be incarnate in contemporary culture; but if it is to be truly Christian, it must be centred on Christ. Catechetics is fundamentally the communication of Jesus Christ. The fault of much past catechetics is not that it tried to teach scholastic theology to anyone, but that it tried to teach a set of abstract propositions instead of trying to communicate Jesus. What Christian catechetics are trying to communicate primarily is not really words, nor even ideas, but Jesus Christ who is the Word and the revelation of God.

For two decades we have been witnessing a reaction against past catechetical approaches that overemphasised the teaching of abstract doctrinal propositions. The Baltimore catechism, for example, while dogmatically sound, leaves much to be desired catechetically. It represents a catechesis that is not truly incarnate in modern culture. The reaction to this lack of catechetical incarnationalism sometimes takes the form of a catechesis that teaches about "life" without any explicit reference to Christ or the Church. The remedy unfortunately is worse than the sickness. Overemphasis on abstract doctrine is not remedied by teaching mere humanism. The answer to overstress on doctrinal propositions is not simply to teach about "life" but to teach Jesus Christ. The fact

75

that religious education has become more life-centred and tries harder to communicate Christ in terms of people's life-experience is, of course, progress. It also has to be said that teaching about "life in depth" or teaching how to be fully and deeply human is good in itself, but it is not the teaching or religion. The answer is not to teach scholastic theology, nor to teach mere humanism, but to base catechesis on the central Christian fact of the interpersonal faith relationship between the person and Jesus Christ. Christianity is not primarily about the doctrine contained in the Council of Trent. Nor is Christianity primarily about life-experience. Christianity is about Christ and how we are, through the world, in relationship with the risen Jesus.

The trouble with both doctrine-centred and life-centred catechetical approaches is that they are content-centred rather than process-oriented. Their content-centredness makes them not only static and culturally inappropriate but also unable to communicate Christ. Catechetics, after all, is an initiation into faith. And this faith is not the faith that is simply an intellectual assent to the truths that God has revealed on the authority of him who can neither deceive nor be deceived. Nor is it just a belief in "life". The faith into which catechetics is an initiation is the living faith of the Gospel. It is a faith that is a loving adherence to the person of Christ.

Jesus Christ is a Person. He cannot be taught as though he were a set of truths or a cluster of insights into "life". The purpose of catechesis is to bring persons to encounter, and to more fully encounter, Jesus — in himself, in his Church, in persons, in experience, in the world. What must be taught, then, are those processes by which Jesus Christ can be met and adhered to, the processes by which he can be known and loved and served. If Jesus is to be known, loved, and served, in himself and in others, the principal processes that are to be learned are processes of understanding and valuing experience in reference to Jesus, processes of prayer, and processes involved in living and working with others in a Christian way.

One set of processes that catechesis should try to inculcate are those processes by which human experience and Christian faith can be understood as integrated and by which daily life can be seen as having a religious value. To do this, catechesis must begin with life-experience, but it cannot end there. It must illuminate the Christian meaning of life-experience by showing how it is related to Jesus Christ.

A second set of processes that catechesis is concerned with are the processes involved in prayer, the processes involved in entering explicitly and consciously into relationship with God. These should be learned in the context of both liturgical and non-liturgical prayer. The processes involved are, as related to God, those of offering, of thanking, of praising, of asking, of loving, of hoping, of trusting. Prayer is an element that is sadly lacking in much contemporary religious education. There are catechists who are embarrassed by prayer. They do not know quite what to do with it, and so they do not do anything with it. Nevertheless, the catechesis of even the smallest child should be ordered to prayer. It is true that Christianity is a religion for adults, but surely it is not *only* for adults. Children have a right to know about Christ and to know how to know him and communicate with him and love him. Children have a right to know about Jesus, and they have a right to be taught how to encounter him as a person, to take him seriously as a person who takes them seriously as persons, to encounter him in prayer. Christian catechesis that does not lead up to and include prayer is simply not Christian.

A third set of processes that catechesis should communicate are the processes that relate to living and working with other persons, the processes of Christian community. These include many of the same basic processes involved in prayer, but with a different reference: loving, trusting, giving, receiving, and so on — but in reference to other persons in the light of Christ.

But what about doctrinal content? And what about the content of daily life-experience? Content should be used pragmatically. It should be used insofar as it helps to effectively inculcate the sets of processes that are involved in attaining an integrated Christian vision of life, in praying, and in living with others in a Christian way. The content of catechesis will include, surely, the truths of Scripture and tradition as well as data from daily life; but all this content will be used functionally — to communicate Jesus Christ in terms of experience.

What catechetics has to learn from listening to and reflecting on the ideas of Teilhard de Chardin can be summarised in a sentence. Religious education must be directed to a full and broad personal union with God in Christ, and through the world.

Prayer for receptivity to the teaching of Jesus

Lord Jesus, teach me your ways. Teach me, so that I can enter more deeply into the processes of prayer that support and nourish my relationships with you. Teach me to pray. Teach me to contemplate you in love and in simplicity, like a child. Teach me to participate more fully in group worship. Teach me to read the Bible slowly and prayerfully. Teach me to contact you, in love, in my prayer. Give me the the knowledge of you, through love — through the love that you have for me and that you pour into my heart — that is the heart of prayer. Teach me to pray.

Teach me, Jesus, to understand and to value myself, the persons around me, and all of reality, in the light of your love. And teach me to understand you and the whole content of my Christian faith in such a way that I know the meaning for my daily life. Teach me how to integrate my everyday experience and my Christian faith.

Teach me also how to enter in a more Christian way into the various human relationships in my life. Teach me to love, to give, to receive, to communicate, to share, to work with others — all in a more Christian way.

And teach me, Jesus, to teach others in whatever ways are appropriate for me. Show me how to guide those for whom I might have responsibility. Help me to teach by how I live, by what I say, by how I respond to people and events. Teach others through me, Lord, by making me a witness to your love, an instrument of your teaching other persons.

Amen.

5
Christian life today

Teilhard's spirituality takes up the traditional, even perennial, tensions in Christian life, but in their contemporary forms — and this is his newness: to name our tensions in the way we experience them, and to show us how to handle them. The fundamental polarities of Christian living have always been the tensions between present and future, doctrine and life, prayer and action, person and community.

Present and future

The present-future polarity, in Teilhard's own spiritual life as revealed in his unpublished retreat notes, as well as in his published writings, takes the shape of the contemporary problem of hope. Teilhard reminds us that we live in the age of the primacy of the future. Mankind as a whole, as never before, has become conscious of itself as a collectivity headed into a future for which it is responsible. In this age of planning for the future, of studying and forecasting the future, of buying on credit and of insurance, of schools seen primarily as preparation for future careers, no wonder we find, as an outstanding characteristic of our times, anxiety. We face the future, and it scares us. The future menaces us with what it might hold. Teilhard analysing modern anxiety, finds that its root lies in what he calls "the sickness of the dead end". Mankind moves with anxiety into a future of increasing organisation, of growing technology, and of evil that has already taken on apocalyptic proportions and that promises even worse wars and oppression and suffering.

But the ultimate and root problem is the problem of the ultimate future. Is this all there is? After the future, then what? Where does the world end, and if — after it — there is nothing, does it really matter whether it ends with a bang or a whimper? Like miners trapped in a mine-shaft, its entrance blocked by an explosion, we are afraid there might be no way out, that human progress might have no ultimately successful outcome, that the future is closed. We find ourselves facing the possibility that, after all, finally, there will be nothing. The sickness of the dead end.

In the life of each of us, the problem of hope in the future can dominate other concerns. What does the future hold for me? I can become anxious looking at the future, because the future looks back blankly, offering me few clues and no real insurance. Ultimately, my anxiety about the future finds its deepest roots in the knowledge that I will die. And after death, what happens to me? Nothing? Again, we meet the sickness of the dead end. Death, for Teilhard, opens out into the "Unknown". In his personal retreat notes for 1939 he writes, "When death approaches, we lose the taste for life, or at least we risk losing it". He writes of his own anxiety in the face of death. "Will Jesus be there? Will he take me or reject me?" (1939 retreat). "Nothing would be difficult *if* one were sure that there is a Jesus on the other side" (1941 retreat). "As if Christ were *not* real for me; should it be normal that Christ leave untouched the sensible surface of anguish and that he work more deeply, never at the level of what is felt and perceived but *beyond* it?" (1942 retreat). He writes of his "physical anxiety" and his "vertigo of fragility and instability" (1945) and of "the old fear: that there is Nothing on the other side" (1949). The problem of the future is a problem of hope.

Hope requires mutuality. I might hope it will not rain on the picnic, but this is only a wish, not real hope. I hope in persons. If I hope I get a ride home after the party, I am hoping that some*one* will give me a ride. So, to hope in the future, I need somehow to see the future in personal terms, as having a face. Further, I need a firm promise, a guarantee that everything will turn out all right in the future, and particularly in the ultimate future, beyond my death and beyond the terminal point of this world.

Teilhard finds these conditions fulfilled in — and fulfilled only in — Jesus Christ risen.

83

The risen Christ holds the future of the universe, and of all mankind, and of each one of us, in his hands. I do not know what the future holds, but I do know who holds the future. Jesus Christ risen holds my future, my family's future, the world's future, hidden in his hands. And, present to me now in my prayer, in the Church, and in a special way in the sacrament of the Eucharist, he makes my future present now in him. So, he stands as the ground of my hope. He gives the future a human face, and he promises me firmly that it will turn out all right.

When Teilhard writes about the "Omega point", borrowing from John's Apocalypse ("I am the Alpha and the Omega"), this is what he means. Jesus risen is the Omega point, the future focal centre of the world's history, of all true progress, and of every human heart. At the end, as the "Omega", stands Jesus Christ risen. We hope in him.

Teilhard had written religious, philosophical and theological essays before the First World War, but they are in a classic mould and unremarkable. During the war, at the front and behind the lines, Teilhard kept his thoughts in a notebook, and the thoughts turned into essays. These essays centre on his insight that Jesus Christ risen is the centre of reality, of the cosmos, of the whole material-spiritual world that we know; and they mark the beginning of Teilhard's truly original thought. During the war, in the midst of death and confusion,

Teilhard found new ways of formulating his hope in the risen Christ.

During the rest of his life, he developed and refined what he had to offer: a formulation of Christian faith that relates that faith to contemporary life, a restating of key Christian truths in a more meaningful and so more livable way. In a changing world, the word of God must continually be brought to new expression, must be adapted and readapted to new generations. This does not mean that God's word should be distorted to suit the hearers, nor watered down to meet modern cravings. It means simply that God's word must be addressed to people. Teilhard had as his life-goal the bringing-to-expression of God's word in the thought-patterns and categories of the contemporary world.

Doctrine and life

This reformulation-of-faith is Teilhard's contribution towards a solution to the problem of the tension between doctrine and life. What does what I believe really have to do with my life? Teilhard wants to show me the *meaning* of what I believe *for* my everyday life. And vice versa: the meaning of my everyday life in the light cast by what I believe.

Since we live in a world perceived as changing, evolving, future-oriented, we need to understand our faith in terms of that perceived world. So Teilhard develops a theory of the evolution of society, and uses that theory to construct a Christology, a theology of Jesus Christ risen as the world's focus. On that Christology, he builds a spirituality of the meaning of all that we do and undergo in this world.

The basic reason for Teilhard's theory of evolution is that he might work out a Christology that speaks to us today, a Christology to serve as the framework for a contemporary Christian spirituality.

Teilhard's theology of Christ risen has the central place in his thoughts. More precisely, the centre of this thought is the faith relationship between the Christian and the risen Christ. And Jesus risen, through this faith relationship that he gives in love, reveals to the Christian the meaning of everyday life. That is, Jesus Christ reveals himself to the Christian, through faith; and the light of that revelation, the Light that Jesus is, shows to the Christian the meaning of his everyday life.

What does the term "Christian faith" mean for Teilhard? What, in the context of Teilhard's Christology and in the context of my daily life, can it mean for me?

For Teilhard, "Christian faith" has the same content as the term "faith" has in the New Testament. "Faith", in the New Testament, has the meaning of adherence in loving trust to the person of Jesus. This faith goes far beyond a mere intellectual assent, beyond the simple recognition of Christian truth. Faith, going beyond the *recognition* of the saving truth of Jesus Christ, embraces him, holds on to him, accepts him wholeheartedly. Faith, then, is the gift of an inter-personal relationship with Jesus, a relationship of love that includes hope, an intimate relationship of loving trust.

In John's gospel, for example, Jesus invites people to have faith in him by "manifesting his glory", by the works that he does and by the words that he speaks. In particular, Jesus' miracles do not in the first place establish his messianic credentials. Rather, they have as their primary purpose to invite us to have faith in Jesus, to adhere in trust to him, to believe in him. As his greatest work, Jesus dies for us and rises from the dead, explicitly inviting us to believe in him risen: "Blessed are those who have not seen and yet believe" (John 20, 29). And whoever believes in Jesus will have life and will rise on the last day (John 6, 40), because Jesus himself is "resurrection and life" (John 11, 25).

Furthermore, Jesus sustains in existence the whole universe. "All things were made through him" (John 1, 3). John's gospel understands Jesus as the Father's creative word, uttered at the beginning of time and now made flesh, entering into the world to save it. Jesus, God's word of salvation to us, saves us through faith, through our trusting adherence to him. And because Jesus *is* the world's meaning, the light of the world, he reveals through faith the meaning for us of the world around us.

Paul's letters express the same idea of salvation through faith in Jesus. The Jesus of

Paul's experience is the risen Jesus who encountered Paul on the road to Damascus, blinding him with light and knocking him down and into a new relationship of faith. This same risen Christ saves us, justifies us, through faith in him; and that faith reconciles us in him with the Father. Through faith I profess and claim Jesus as the Lord of my life.

Since he whom I profess as my Lord holds in his hands the whole universe, is the Lord of all things, my faith relationship with him shows me the meaning of all reality. Jesus risen, who reconciles me through faith to himself and in him to the Father, is reconciling the whole world to himself and in himself to the Father. This is history's meaning because it is God's plan for the world, "a plan for the fullness of time, to unite all things in him" (Ephesians 1, 10). Christ risen, Lord of all, and my Lord, reveals to me through my faith relationship with him: who he is for me, and who I am for him, and what the world is for me in him.

"Faith", for Teilhard, has the same meaning as it does for John and for Paul and for the entire New Testament, when Teilhard uses the word to indicate Christian faith. Christian faith includes a vision of reality and a programme for living, but it goes beyond both of these in a personal adherence to the risen Christ. More exactly, the Christian faith vision finds its roots and its coherence in the relationship of faith; and Christian life takes its meaning as well as its force from faith relationship with Jesus Christ risen.

What, then, is the meaning of my Christian faith in the light of my everyday life? What does my religious faith mean for my daily life? This: my Christian faith calls me to live my everyday life in a greater awareness of its meaning in Jesus Christ, to live it at a deeper level in him, to participate with a clearer consciousness and a more loving involvement in the world, which holds together and centres on Jesus risen.

The meaning of my Christian faith for my ongoing life of every day is that my faith calls me to follow Jesus. My faith *is* the following of Jesus, united to him, with and through and in him. To follow Jesus, for Teilhard, means to do what Jesus did: to enter fully into the world, as Jesus did by his incarnation; to live out in love that involvement in the world, as Jesus did during his life on earth; and to carry the cross of the weight of the world, as Jesus did in his passion. Christian faith calls to, means, deeper and fuller and more loving commitment to the world. Commitment to the world — not to the world of sin, to the world under God's judgement, to the world that retrogresses away from the reconciliation and the unity of all things in Christ risen. Rather: commitment to the world that moves towards Jesus Christ, towards its future focal point who is the Person in whom it holds together and who gives it its meaning and value.

What is the meaning of my everyday life in the light of my Christian faith? What does my life mean in the light of the Light of the world? Jesus, through his faith relationship with me, lights up my life and reveals to me what my life means, what I mean, what the world around means for me in him.

The meaning of the world around me is that it is centred on the risen Christ and moving towards a greater completeness in him. The meaning of my life is that all that I do that is positive contributes, somehow, to the progressive unification of all things in Christ, the unification that is God's plan for the world. And the meaning of my own existence is that I am called to follow Jesus, to enter always more fully and in faith into personal relationship with Jesus Christ, a relationship that exists in and through the world I live in.

Where does Christian doctrine come into the picture? What is the meaning for me of the doctrine of Christianity? And how does Christian teaching illuminate the meaning of my life? *Through faith.* Through my adherence in trust and in faith to Jesus Christ risen. Jesus contains in himself all authentic Christian teaching. All Christian revelation is contained in him, summed up in him. Furthermore, no Christian doctrine means anything apart from Jesus; separated from him, any Christian teaching becomes a dead letter.

Jesus Christ, who died for our sins and who rose again and who is present to us now in our lives in this world, either is everything, or he is nothing. Either he is Lord of the universe and all that it holds, or he is Lord of nothing. Either all of reality, including myself and my situation in the world, finds its meaning in him; or else it has no meaning beyond itself.

For the Christian, Jesus Christ is everything. The Christian puts all his eggs in one basket: personal faith relationship with Christ. He puts all his money on what he knows is the one winning number: Jesus risen. The Christian finds in Jesus both the meaning of Christian doctrine and the meaning of life.

Prayer and action

Teilhard sees as the chief religious problem of today the apparent conflict between prayer and action. He observes that most Christians today feel, at least to some degree, torn between an "upward" impulse towards God of prayer and worship, and a "forward" impulse towards involvement in the world. The Christian of this century believes in God; he also believes in the world around him, in his family, friends, work. And he finds himself pulled in two directions, upward towards God and forward into the world around him and its future that he helps to build. Teilhard calls this "the problem of the two faiths". How can we bring the "Upward" and the "Forward" into synthesis?

The perennial Christian polar tension between action and contemplation takes the shape today of a conflict between a "vertical" faith in God and a "horizonal" faith in the world, in the human, in the future. Teilhard responds to that ancient problem in its new form by showing us that the God of the Upward and the God of the Forward are the same risen Jesus Christ who is "ahead" as much as he is "above". Because Christ risen is the future focal centre, the apex, of the world's movement into the future, I am called to enter deeply into the world, to be involved in the world *because* I am a Christian. And because the world is centred on Christ, everything I do in that world has meaning in him. My "action" as well as my "contemplation" has religious significance. The risen Christ, then, acts in my life as a living and personal principle of synthesis. He gathers me together. He knits up the frazzled parts of my life. He heals me, makes me whole, integral — gives my life integrity. Jesus risen pulls together the "vertical" and the "horizontal" and all the strands in my life so that, in him, my life holds together in unity. He does this in terms of my daily existence lived out in faith, lived out in personal adherence to him.

The centre of my faith relationship with Jesus Christ is my personal prayer. Here, in my personal prayer, my relation to Christ finds its most intense form, its most human conscious moments. And it is in my personal prayer that Jesus Christ most acts to pull me together to centre me on himself. He is interested in everything in my life, even the most banal or seemingly uninteresting items. He cares about my financial worries, about difficulties in my work, about my health — about all the things that I worry about. Whatever preoccupies me, Jesus — because it preoccupies me — cares about it in my life. Because he loves me. Whoever attracts or repels me or seriously occupies my mind or my heart for any reason — that person and my relation to him or to her concerns Jesus; because I concern him.

His aim is to recapitulate all things in my life under one head, under one Lord, himself. He wants to bring everything and everyone in my life, in so far as I am in relationship with those people or with those things, under his lordship. Jesus wants to integrate into the central and fundamental relationship in my life — my relationship with him — all the other relationships, of whatever kind, that exist in my life. He desires to centre all my relationships around my central relationship with him so that he can vitalise and deepen and fill with his love my whole life. He does this chiefly in my prayer; and he calls me to cooperate, to actively participate in his project to get me and everything in my life together. How can I do this?

I can bring my cares, worries, preoccupations, attractions and repulsions to him, give them over to him, put them in his hands. I can put whatever is on my mind in Jesus' hands: my anger, my weight problem, my fear, a friend, tomorrow and what might happen. I can put things explicitly under his lordship. I can bring all the "action" in my life into my contemplation. Sitting at Jesus' feet, looking at him, choosing "the better part" and doing "the one thing necessary", I can cooperate with Jesus' project — the integration of my life — by bringing to him all the elements of my life that tend to remain outside the zone of his love for me, outside the zone of our relationship.

My distractions in prayer give me clues. Whatever distracts me in prayer lies somehow outside the framework of my relation to God. Otherwise, the thought of it would not be a distraction but a prayer. The fact that thought of a certain person *distracts* me in my prayer indicates that the person, in some way, distracts me from the Lord; there is something in my relation to that person that needs straightening out, rectification. In some way, that relationship is not fully integrated into my prayerful relation to Jesus Christ.

What can I do? I can make the content of my distraction the subject of my prayer. I can pray about what distracts me, making a prayer out of the distraction. And in that way, I help the Lord to get my life together, centred on him. I cooperate with Jesus' work of uniting all my actions and interests and cares in the framework of my contemplation. In this way, by putting everything in Jesus' hands, by putting everything "in Christ", I can find everything in him. I can understand my whole life as in synthesis in Jesus Christ, given unity through my relation to him. I can find all things in Christ.   And, therefore, I am able to find Christ in all things.

The four-century old Jesuit tradition of "contemplation in action" and of "finding God in all things" goes back to the Jesuit founder, Saint Ignatius of Loyola. Pierre Teilhard de Chardin, as a Jesuit, was steeped in this tradition. He lived it. His idea of uniting prayer and action in terms of union with Christ is, basically, according to the deepest Jesuit tradition. It might be said that Teilhard adds a certain Christocentrism to the idea of "contemplating God in action" so as to "find God in all things". However, the evidence indicates that, at least in the personal spiritual life of Ignatius of Loyola, the concept was already thoroughly Christocentric; to "find God in all things" seems to have meant for Ignatius, to "find Jesus Christ in all things".

Teilhard views all creation as holding together in Jesus risen. The risen Christ exercises a universal influence of love over all creation and over every individual creature. In fact, Teilhard's theology of creation is really a Christology of creation. There is a direct relation from every creature to Jesus Christ risen, because it is of his loving influence that the creature continues to exist.

Because all creation exists "in Christ", Teilhard can find Christ in all creation and, in some way, in every creature and in every action and in every event. And so, Teilhard teaches me to extend my contemplation outside my prayer time, and to live contemplatively, finding Jesus in all that I meet and in all that I do.

Because he is the Lord and the Centre of all of it.

Person and community

Just as Teilhard finds in the risen Christ the principle of hope in the future, the solution to the tension between faith and doctrine, and the synthesis of the "vertical" and the "horizonal", so too he finds in Jesus risen the resolution of the tension between the individual person and the community. We are used to thinking of "person" and "community" as opposed concepts; Teilhard shows how they are correlative and complementary. In any biological unity, a living body for example, the parts are more highly differentiated according as the body is more highly organised; the human body, highly organised, has greatly differentiated and specialised organs. So too, on any team — medical, or teaching, or football — the team members find themselves differentiated according to function on the team, precisely in terms of the team's functional unity. Union differentiates.

When persons are united by love in any form (married love, friendship, patriotism, devotion to a common cause), when they are united precisely as persons, then they find themselves differentiated as persons, personalised. Union differentiates, and union of love personalises. We find ourselves and we grow as persons through entering lovingly into community with others.

The problem is loving. Teilhard has no illusions about our natural egoism, our innate selfishness. We cannot really love as we should; we love possessively, selfishly, using one another; we love not with an open hand that leaves others free, but grasping and manipulating. The answer to the tension between person and community is love, and the answer to our inability to love well or even adequately is Jesus Christ, whom Teilhard calls "the King and Centre of love". If union of love personalises, then the risen Christ, who loves me and who died for me, unites me to himself in love, personalises me, helps me to grow in my capacity to love and to receive love. Uniting each of us to himself, he makes us one in him, the Person at the centre of every true community of love.

But not all community is loving. Many kinds of organised human community stifle the individual person, limit personal freedom, quench hope and love. Not every human union personalises.

Only where there is love, a union of heart to heart, can union personalise. A prison has a disciplined and highly organised group of people, but it is not a personalising community.

Union personalises when the persons come together centre to centre, as *subjects*. When they treat one another as persons, as subjects. When they act with love towards one another. Where persons treat one another without love, as objects, they depersonalise one another. They destroy one another rather than build up.

Prayers

We can pray about the four fundamental tensions of Christian life that this chapter has considered, the tensions between: person and community, life and doctrine, prayer and action, present and future.

1. Prayer that my relationships with others may be more filled with love: Lord Jesus, centre on yourself all the personal relationships in my life. I give them to you; I put them in your hands, under your lordship. Integrate them into your loving relationship with me. I offer to you, one by one, the persons that I love, that I live with, that I work with, my family and my friends, one by one, as I pray for each of these persons, and fill that relationship with your love; strengthen it, deepen it, transform it, straighten out whatever you see in that relationship that needs correction. Make every relationship in my life a personalising one. Lord Jesus, I offer to you also those persons in my life with whom I have difficulty. I offer to you one at a time those persons towards whom I feel resentment or anger, who have hurt me or saddened me or opposed me. I forgive them, with your help, one by one. And I ask you, Jesus, to enter into each one of those relationships, to transform it. Amen.

2. Prayer for light: Lord Jesus, shine the light of your love in my life. Help me to see more clearly, to integrate in my understanding and in a single vision my Christian faith and

my perception of myself and the world around
me. Shine the light of your love, Lord, in my
mind and in my heart so that I see everything
— all that I believe and all that I live — in
terms of you, of your love and care, of your
presence. You, Lord Jesus, are the Lord of all
things. Help me to understand that. Amen.

3.   Prayer for integration of life: Lord
Jesus, centre me on yourself. Pull me together;
make me whole; heal me by your personal and
forgiving love of me. You call me by name,
and I come to you. I bring you everything in
my life, all my thoughts, words, actions, joys
and sufferings. I put them in your hands for
your blessing. And right now, Lord, in this
moment, I place firmly in your hands what
is on my mind in this present moment. Amen.

4.   Prayer of hope: Jesus, I put all my hope
in you. You are the ground of my hope.

I repent of my sins, Lord, and I am sorry
for them. But now I accept your loving mercy,
your compassionate forgiveness, and put my
sinful past behind me.

Take away my fear of the future, my worry
and distress in the face of what might happen.
Fill me with your perfect love that casts out all
fear.

You hold my whole future, tomorrow and
next week and the months and years that
follow, completely in your hands. I do not know
what my future holds; but I know that you
hold my future. I trust you, and I trust your
love for me.

You have taught me, Jesus, that the gate to salvation is narrow, and that few enter through that narrow gate. I know, Lord Jesus, that you yourself are the gate to salvation, that you are the Way I must go, the gate I must pass through.

I give you my heart. Give me a strong hope, a firm trust in you and in the power of your love for me. Jesus, Lord of my future, I put my trust in you. Amen.

SELECTED BIBLIOGRAPHY

Books by Pierre Teilhard de Chardin

THE DIVINE MILIEU (also published under the French title, *Le Milieu Divin*), Collins, London, and Harper and Row, New York, 1960. This is Teilhard's masterpiece of Christian spirituality. It needs to be complemented, however, by reading some of his more theological essays or by reading one or more of the theological commentaries on his thought.

HYMN OF THE UNIVERSE, Collins, London, and Harper and Row, New York, 1965. A collection of poetic essays, written before Teilhard had clearly formulated his ideas, valuable especially for showing the relationship between Jesus Christ and the world, a relationship centred in the sacrament of the Eucharist.

TOWARD THE FUTURE, Collins, London, and Harcourt Brace Jovanovich Inc., New York, 1975. Theological essays with the general theme of a future-oriented Christianity in a world headed towards Christ-Omega.

THE HEART OF MATTER, Collins, London, and Harcourt Brace Jovanovich, New York, 1978. Essays in spirituality, including two key essays, "The Heart of Matter" (an autobiographical description of the progress of Teilhard's thought and spiritual life) and "Le Christique" (a dense and powerful Christological statement).

CHRISTIANITY AND EVOLUTION, Collins, London, and Harcourt Brace Jovanovich, New York, 1969. Theological essays on Christianity in general, almost all of them important and interesting.

101

Books about Teilhard de Chardin's thought

ALL THINGS IN CHRIST: TEILHARD DE CHARDIN'S SPIRITUALITY, by Robert Faricy, S.J.; Collins, London, and Winston, Minneapolis, 1981. Uses Teilhard's personal notebooks and retreat notes as well as his books and essays. Contains chapters on the Heart of Jesus in Teilhard's life and writings, on ecumenism, on the cross, and on Teilhard's eschatology.

TOWARDS A NEW MYSTICISM, by Ursula King; Collins, London, and Seabury Press, New York, 1981. Studies Teilhard's ideas especially regarding non-Christian religions.

TEILHARD DE CHARDIN'S THEOLOGY OF THE CHRISTIAN IN THE WORLD, by Robert Faricy, S.J.; Sheed and Ward, New York, 1967. Teilhard's spiritual theology; an introduction to and overview of his religious thought.

TEILHARD DE CHARDIN AND THE MYSTERY OF CHRIST, by Christopher Mooney; Collins, London, and Harper and Row, New York, 1966. An outstanding study of Teilhard's Christology, and an excellent introduction to his ideas.

TEILHARD — A BIOGRAPHY, by Mary and Ellen Lukas; Collins, London, and Doubleday and Co., New York, 1977. The best and most complete biography of Teilhard.

BUILDING GOD'S WORLD, by Robert Faricy, S.J.; Dimension Books, Denville, N.J., 1976. A Teilhardian theology of Christian involvement in the world.

CHRIST AND THE UNIVERSE, by Robert Hale, O.S.B. Cam.; Franciscan Herald Press, Chicago, 1973. A scholarly study of Teilhard's theological cosmology.